CHIMPANZEE RESCUE

CHIMPANZEE RESCUE

Changing the Future for Endangered Wildlife

PATRICIA BOW

FIREFLY BOOKS

A Firefly Book

Published by Firefly Books Ltd. 2004

First printing

PUBLISHER CATALOGING-IN-PUBLICATION DATA (U.S.)
Bow, Patricia.
Chimpanzee rescue : changing the future for endangered wildlife / Patricia Bow. –1st ed.
[64] p. : col. photos. ; cm. (Firefly animal rescue)
Includes index.
Summary: Provides details and facts about chimpanzees and bonobos, their endangerment and extinction, and a range of
conservation programs to save them. Includes profiles of individual conservationists and chimp populations.
ISBN 1-55297-909-1
ISBN 1-55297-908-3 (pbk.)
1. Chimpanzee — Juvenile literature. 2. Endangered species – Juvenile literature. I. Title. II. Series.
599.885 dc22 QL737.P96.B69 2004

LIBRARY AND ARCHIVES CANADA CATALOGUING IN PUBLICATION
Bow, Patricia, 1946–
Chimpanzee rescue : changing the future for endangered
wildlife / Patricia Bow.
(Firefly animal rescue)
ISBN 1-55297-909-1 (bound).— ISBN 1-55297-908-3 (pbk.)
1. Chimpanzees—Juvenile literature. 2. Bonobo—Juvenile literature.
3. Endangered species—Juvenile literature. I. Title. II. Series.

QL737.P96B69 2004   j599.885   C2004-903041-8

Published in the United States by
Firefly Books (U.S.) Inc.
P.O. Box 1338, Ellicott Station
Buffalo, New York 14205

Published in Canada by
Firefly Books Ltd.
66 Leek Crescent
Richmond Hill, Ontario L4B 1H1

Design: Ingrid Paulson
Maps: Roberta Cooke

Printed in Canada by Friesens, Altona, Manitoba

The Publisher acknowledges the financial support of the Government of Canada
through the Book Publishing Industry Development Program for its publishing activities.

TABLE OF CONTENTS

OUR COUSINS, THE CHIMPS

Six or seven million years ago, a common ancestor of humans and chimpanzees roamed across Africa. Although evolution has led us along separate paths, humans are still closer to chimps than to any other mammal. Scientists look to the chimps for clues as they explore how our remote ancestors lived. No wonder the chimpanzee holds a special place in our imagination.

A century ago, as many as two million chimpanzees inhabited Africa. Today, probably fewer than 200,000 remain in the wild. Some estimates put the figure as low as 110,000. Up to 3,500 chimps live in captivity, including nearly 1,200 in zoos. The animals are extinct in five of the 25 countries where they once lived, and reduced to scattered remnants in half a dozen others.

Chimpanzees and the closely related bonobos, along with gorillas and orangutans, are great apes. They are part of the primate order of mammals, which also includes humans, monkeys, and about 200 smaller species. But all four subspecies of chimpanzee (*Pan troglodytes*) and the single bonobo species (*Pan paniscus*) are endangered.

Still, despite all that human beings have done to chimpanzees, the animals are not yet doomed. It's often said that when you look into the eyes of a chimpanzee, you can't help but feel a flash of recognition. Thousands of scientists, wildlife officials and zoo and sanctuary workers have looked into those eyes. Their dedication and hard work—along with a lot of help from animal lovers around the world—may be enough to keep our closest cousins alive.

WHERE DO CHIMPANZEES LIVE?

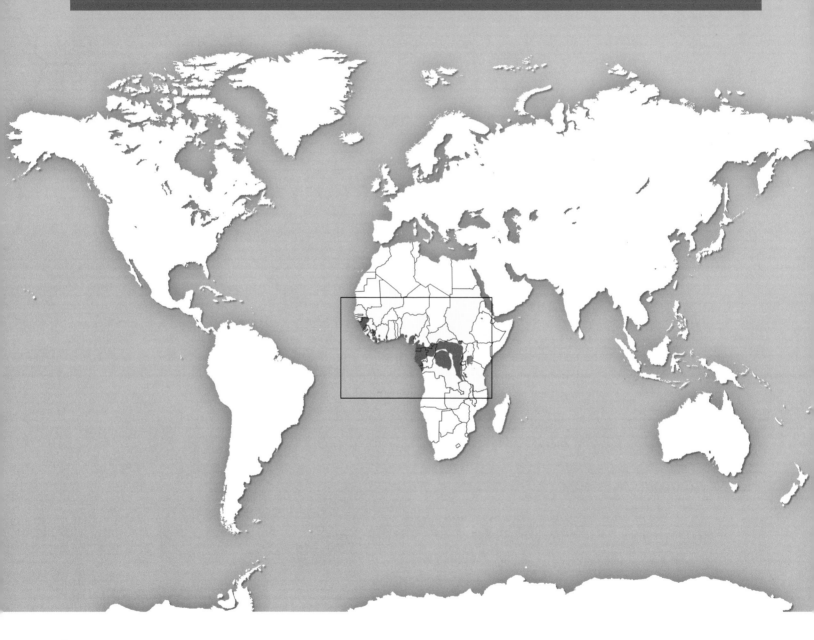

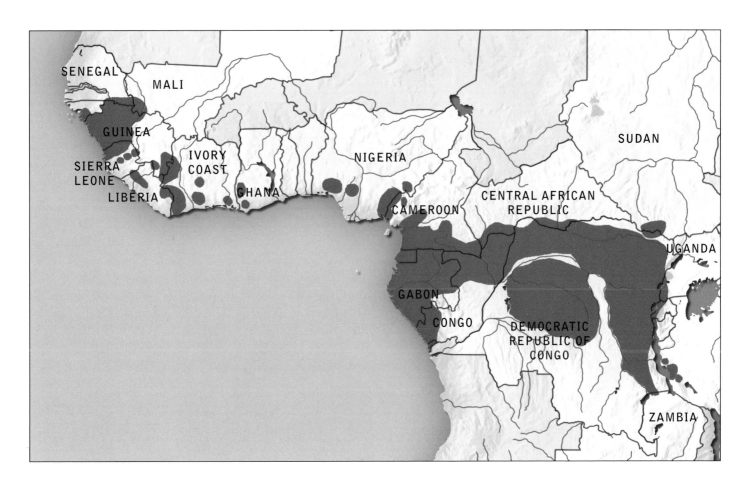

Chimpanzees live in 20 countries within a belt of tropical rainforest that
stretches across Africa's middle. The four subspecies, each with its own
slight physical differences, can be found in West, Central and East Africa,
and along the Nigeria-Cameroon border.

Cameroon, the Democratic Republic of Congo, Ivory Coast, and Gabon have the
largest chimp populations. Smaller groups live in Angola, Burundi, the Central
African Republic, the Republic of Congo, Equatorial Guinea, Ghana, Guinea, Liberia,
Mali, Nigeria, Rwanda, Senegal, Sierra Leone, Sudan, Tanzania and Uganda.

Bonobos are confined to the Democratic Republic of Congo.

9

THE STORY SO FAR

Our knowledge of chimpanzees has grown enormously in the last 40 years because of scientists like Jane Goodall, who began her research in Tanzania in 1960. Goodall's reports of human-like behavior in chimps—making and using tools, hunting cooperatively, waging war and showing signs of friendship and love—were both controversial and groundbreaking.

∧ Chimpanzees like Enos—not humans—were among the first earthlings in space.

From the 1950s to early '70s, thousands of chimps were exported from Africa, to be used for lab research as well as entertainment. Laws have since slowed the live trade, although it does continue illegally. Today, the chief threats to the chimpanzee population are large-scale logging and overhunting by humans.

In the late 1990s, conservation groups that had been working quietly for decades went into high gear, as chimpanzee numbers slid faster and faster. The turn of the millennium brought more laws and new international efforts to protect chimps and other apes. The race against extinction was on.

1960 Jane Goodall starts her research at Gombe Stream Reserve, Tanzania.
1961 A five-year-old chimp named Enos orbits Earth in a spacecraft, three months earlier than the first human in space.
1966 Washoe, a female chimpanzee, begins learning American Sign Language.
1969 The Chimpanzee Rehabilitation Project, the first of 16 African sanctuaries for orphaned chimps, is established in Gambia.

1973 The International Primate Protection League is founded to expose conditions in the live primate trade.

1975 American scientists announce that humans and chimps share 98.6 percent of their DNA. Both chimpanzees and bonobos are classified as threatened.

1976 The U.S. stops importing wild chimps and bonobos, in keeping with its Endangered Species Act.

1984 Scientists discover that chimpanzees can be infected with HIV, the virus that causes AIDS. Soon afterward, a breeding program is set up in the United States to supply chimps for AIDS research.

1988 The chimpanzee's status is downgraded from threatened to endangered.

1997 *Pan troglodytes vellerosus*, found in Nigeria and Cameroon, is the most recent chimp subspecies to be identified.

1999 New Zealand is the first country to pass laws banning research on chimps. The Netherlands follows in 2002, Sweden in 2003.

2000 African sanctuaries form the Pan-African Sanctuary Alliance to coordinate their efforts as the numbers of orphaned and homeless primates rise. The U.S. passes two new acts to help fund chimp conservation.

2001 The United Nations creates the Great Ape Survival Project (GRASP) to help African countries manage chimp conservation plans.

2003 Ebola, a deadly virus that also affects humans, devastates chimp populations in Central Africa.

∧ At first, many other scientists scorned Jane Goodall's personal approach to her chimpanzee research subjects.

SHRINKING FORESTS

Chimpanzees and bonobos are mostly arboreal, which means they prefer to live in trees. Their long, strong arms are perfectly adapted for scrambling up trees and swinging from branch to branch. Trees provide the fruit, leaves and buds that make up a large part of their diet. At night, for safety, they build nests in the upper limbs.

Bonobos are almost entirely creatures of the deep forest, while chimps live in a range of habitats, from dense rainforest to open woodlands to dry grasslands—but they never venture far from the shelter of trees.

And the trees are disappearing. The tropical rainforest that once blanketed Central and West Africa shrank by 78,000 square miles (200,000 km²) in the 1990s. At this rate, by 2030, only about eight percent of the chimpanzee's remaining habitat will be undisturbed forest.

They never venture far from the shelter of trees.

Where human populations are on the rise, forests—including protected reserves—are being cleared illegally for farmland, cattle-grazing land and firewood. But commercial logging and mining have done the most damage.

Take for example coltan mining. Coltan is a mineral used to make electronic parts for laptop computers, pagers, and cell phones. When large deposits of the mineral were discovered in the Democratic Republic of Congo in the late 1990s, more than 10,000 miners flooded into protected wilderness areas, including Kahuzi-Biega National Park, home to many rare plants and animals. This mining led to polluted streams, clear-cut forest areas, and the killing of thousands of animals, including gorillas and chimpanzees, for food.

< Illegal logging in the African rainforest is a multi-million-dollar industry. The fall of gigantic trees, like this one in Gabon, also destroys the homes of chimpanzees and other animals.

13

LOVE AND WAR IN THE RAINFOREST

Chimpanzees have what scientists call a "fusion-fission" society. This means that they live in large communities of 20 to 100 that are constantly breaking up and coming together again. Individuals or small groups go off to forage on their own, returning hours or even days later. And they cover a lot of ground: an average community needs four to 20 square miles (10 to 50 km²) of forest to roam.

Adult males spend most of their time together. Grooming, hunting, sharing food, fighting and making up are all part of a constant jockeying for position. The leader, usually the strongest and most aggressive, is called the alpha male.

Male chimpanzees regularly patrol the borders of their territories and often engage in bloody battles.

Male chimpanzees regularly patrol the borders of their territories and often engage in bloody battles with the males of the next territory. In Tanzania, Jane Goodall has reported entire communities being stalked, driven off or wiped out, one by one, by a neighboring community.

Females rarely take part in border wars or hunting parties. Typically, when a female reaches maturity, she leaves home. Rather than mate with close male relatives, she travels into foreign territory to find a mate and bear young. This keeps chimp populations genetically healthy.

Chimpanzees spend almost all their time together in small groups, grooming each >
other, sharing food, playing, and squabbling. The mother-child bond can last a lifetime.

The shrinking of Africa's forests does more than restrict the chimps' freedom. It promotes chimp wars by forcing neighboring communities to live closer together. And it leaves the animals isolated in islands of forest surrounded by only farmland and open grassland. Chimpanzees will rarely leave the safety of the trees to cross wide stretches of open land, so females in these areas must stay home and mate with close relatives. This is called inbreeding, and it tends to produce offspring that are smaller, weaker and less disease-resistant.

In some African countries, including Guinea, Uganda and Tanzania, corridors of trees are being planted to reconnect scattered chimp groups. These plantings are large, expensive projects, and require the cooperation of everyone—from small farmers to national governments. But, short of preserving all chimp habitat forever, corridors may offer the best strategy for keeping chimpanzee communities alive and healthy.

The chimpanzees of the Bossou Hills in Guinea, West Africa, are living in a slowly shrinking prison. No new chimps have come to this community in more than 20 years. Without new blood, fewer healthy babies will be born, and the population's chances of survival will plummet.

He knew it wouldn't be easy.

But not if Tetsuro Matsuzawa can help it. Matsuzawa is a primatologist— a scientist who studies primates—from Kyoto University in Japan, and he leads a field study that began at Bossou in 1976. These chimps belong to the western subspecies *Pan troglodytes verus*, which now number fewer than 25,000. The small group at Bossou —of which no more than 20 remain—became famous in the early 1980s when scientists discovered they use stone tools to crack oil-palm nuts.

Just two and a half miles (4 km) from Bossou lie the Nimba Mountains, home to about 250 chimpanzees. But the Bossou chimpanzees have never been known to cross the open grassland. Matsuzawa's plan was to extend the forest all the way to Nimba. He knew it wouldn't be easy. To create a passage 325

Hundreds of chimpanzees make their home in Guinea's Nimba Mountains.   >

This adult female chimpanzee is using a stone hammer to crack open an oil-palm nut on a stone anvil. A young chimp learns the skill by watching and imitating its mother.

yards (300 m) wide would take about 48,000 seedlings, set 16 feet (5 m) apart. "No one, including my colleagues and students, thought the project was possible," Matsuzawa admits.

In January 1997, he planted a nursery outside the forest—and let the chimpanzees choose the trees. "We had the idea of using chimpanzee feces," he says, explaining that the droppings contained seeds from the fruits the chimps preferred. When the seedlings were two years old, Matsuzawa and his helpers planted them across the savanna, beside a stream. The dry season brought fire, but some of the seedlings survived, and the team planted more.

This family of chimpanzees living in their home forest in Bossou have a brighter future with the planting of a passageway across the savanna.

Today, a chain of small groves of trees, some 16 feet (5 m) high, stretches across the plain between Bossou and Nimba. The patches will form a continuous green corridor in a few years.

> But the chimpanzees have decided not to wait. "In January 2003, when I visited Bossou," Matsuzawa says, "we confirmed that the chimps had crossed through the corridor and stayed two nights on the opposite side."

The chimps are still living in their home forest, but they are no longer cut off from others of their kind. Thanks to a green passage across the brown savanna, the Bossou community now has a future.

When Lee White was a boy, a chimpanzee named Cedric made a deep impression on him—with his teeth. The family had moved to Uganda from England and adopted the baby chimp when his first owners left the country. "I tried to teach—well, force—him to ride my bicycle, and he bit me."

> "I tried to teach—well, force—him to ride my bicycle, and he bit me."

But that painful incident was balanced by moments of wonder, like the first time White heard a "pant-hoot," the loud, excited call that chimps make when finding food or meeting others. "One of my earliest memories is seeing—and hearing—a group of chimps pant-hooting high in a tree in Budongo Forest, in Uganda, where my father had taken me to collect butterflies."

In 1997, as a Wildlife Conservation Society scientist, White studied the impact of logging in Gabon's Lopé Reserve, home to gorillas, elephants, leopards and 3,000 chimpanzees of the central subspecies, *Pan troglodytes troglodytes*. He found that even when logging was done carefully, with only 10 percent of an area cut at a time, chimpanzees were being put in serious peril. When logging machines thundered through a forest, communities of panicked chimps would flee into the next territory, only to be attacked by neighboring chimps defending their border. Four out of five combatants died.

Gabon was once home to a large percentage of Africa's chimps, but by 1997, that population had fallen to 30,000. In that decade, most of Gabon's once-protected rainforest had been opened to lumber companies after the country's main source of wealth, oil, declined in price. White predicted the chimp population could drop to 10,000 if logging continued.

In Gabon's Lopé Reserve, logging companies and conservationists have cooperated to save much of the forest—and its thriving chimpanzee population.

But he understood the economic need. So, while some conservationists called for an immediate logging ban, White spoke to timber-company managers and government officials and worked out a compromise. In July 2000, a tract of valuable okoumé trees on the edge of the Lopé Reserve was traded to the loggers for a smaller block of upland forest—as well as a promise to stop logging on the rest of the reserve.

Even better news: in 2002, the work of Lee White and others encouraged the government of Gabon to establish 13 national parks—covering 10 percent of the country's area—where all wildlife will be protected from logging. Hearing that announcement, White says, now ranks among his most unforgettable moments.

TOO CLOSE FOR COMFORT

Africa's present human population of 850 million is expected to double by 2050. With more and more people living close to chimp habitat, conflicts will increase. And when chimps and humans clash, it's almost always the chimps that lose.

Nearly half of the people in Africa live on a dollar or less a day. War and widespread diseases such as AIDS make life even harder for many rural Africans. It's understandable that desperate people don't worry much about the future of the forests they cut for crops and firewood, or the protected status of the chimpanzees they kill for meat. This is especially true when chimps and people are competing for the same food.

Unlike most primates, chimps are omnivorous—they will eat eggs, termites and the occasional small animal as well as the fruit, leaves, nuts and other plant matter that make up most of their diet. When farmers plant crops close to the forest, chimps are likely to raid them. Corn, sugar cane, bananas and beehive honey are favorite targets. Chimps that are caught in the act are likely to be shot.

Chimps are often the victims even in countries like Uganda, where humans don't usually eat apes. When they encounter traps set for other creatures, chimps are often crippled—and a crippled chimp will not live long.

The ideal solution is to separate the species completely, but that's not always possible. Part of the answer may be ecotourism—well-managed tours that bring small numbers of people to chimpanzee communities.

∧ This baby gorilla, like many chimpanzees and bonobos, most likely lost its mother to human hunters.

< Tourists come from around the world to get a glimpse of chimpanzees at home. When it's done right, ecotourism raises money for conservation and creates jobs.

23

DANGEROUS COMPANY

Roughly six million years ago, early humans and chimpanzees began to evolve separately. But we haven't grown all that far apart. Some scientists now include chimps, bonobos, gorillas and orangutans with humans in the family Hominidae.

We share between 95 and 99 percent of our DNA—the basis of genetic identity—with chimps and bonobos. We also share some blood groups; it's even possible for a human to receive a blood transfusion from a chimp.

This may account for some of the ways in which chimps resemble us. Chimpanzees have learned to eat healing plants when they are sick, and to make tools of wood and stone. Bonobos may place twig and leaf trail markers in the forest for others to follow.

The species' closeness means that diseases can pass easily between them. The AIDS virus was originally passed to humans from chimpanzees, probably when hunters came in contact with infected blood. The deadly Ebola virus was spread in the same way.

Chimps, in turn, can die of human diseases like tuberculosis, leprosy, measles, mumps, chickenpox, rubella, polio and whooping cough. Even flu can kill chimpanzees. Eleven chimpanzees died of flu in 1996 in Gombe National Park, Tanzania, after a field worker regularly handed them food.

Primatologists are calling for stricter health standards for researchers and tourists. At some field study sites, researchers must be vaccinated against a long list of diseases, from yellow fever to meningitis. And they are warned to stay at least 16 feet (5 m) away from the chimps.

∧ An orphaned baby chimpanzee is tested for SIV, the ape form of HIV-AIDS. Many diseases can pass between apes and humans.

All the great apes form close bonds with their children. This bonobo mother and   > child are enjoying a moment of carefree play.

In Budongo Forest, western Uganda, scientists are working with the government and villagers to ease friction between chimpanzees and humans.

∧ Chimpanzees are often maimed by wire snares set for other animals.

Budongo Forest is home to some 580 of Uganda's 5,000 chimpanzees, members of the eastern subspecies, *Pan troglodytes schweinfurthii*. Roughly 25,000 people live in villages and farms around the forest edge. Some set snares in the forest, illegally, for duikers (a kind of antelope) or wild pigs. They don't target chimpanzees—most Ugandans don't eat apes—but chimps often get caught anyway.

"Snaring cripples and kills more chimps than all other threats put together," says Vernon Reynolds, head of the Budongo Forest Project. "It has mushroomed in the last 15 years, with the boom in population around Budongo." A snared chimp can pull free, but may be left with wire twisted around its hand or foot, and may die painfully if the wound becomes infected.

One solution is to pay hunters for removing the snares instead of setting them. By 2003, Budongo had four snare removers at work. On a single day in July they brought in 64 traps. To reinforce this program, two Ugandan educators carry the pro-chimpanzee message to the villages. "We have sensitized people to the chimp problem in our area," Reynolds says. "Many now sympathize with us."

Bonobos, too, fall foul of snares. Missing the fingers of one hand, this bonobo will have a hard time climbing trees and finding food.

Still, sometimes the best solution is simply to put a little space between chimps and humans. In May 2003, a chimp named Jambo was speared next to a field of sugar-cane, which is an irresistible crop for chimps, especially when planted along the forest edge. Jambo's death was a blow to his community—he was its third-ranked male—and to researchers who had been watching him for 12 years.

But Jambo's death did have one positive outcome. The Budongo Forest Project convinced the sugar company to clear a 55-yard (50 m) buffer zone between the fields and the forest. The cleared area may keep the chimps out of the sugar fields in future—and keep them alive.

Vernon Reynolds saw his first wild chimpanzee in Budongo Forest in 1962. He and his wife, Frankie, both fresh out of London University, were hoping to trace the beginnings of human behavior in the social lives and habits of our nearest relatives.

∧ This young chimp may live to be 50 — if he can live safely with his human neighbors.

Until that time, most chimpanzee studies had been carried out in zoos, and almost nothing was known about how the animals lived in the wild. Along with Jane Goodall and a handful of others, Frankie and Vernon Reynolds were among the first scientists to study chimpanzees in the rainforest.

Those eight months in Budongo Forest in 1962 left Vernon entranced with the chimps, and angered by the ways humans treated them. He saw the injuries inflicted by snares, and so began dismantling them. At a time when almost everyone believed that animals existed for the good of human beings, he advised that no more apes should be exported from Africa to zoos or for medical research. As early as 1967, he predicted that the great apes would die out if humans continued to exploit them.

In 1990, Vernon Reynolds returned to Uganda to lead the Budongo Forest Project. A decade later it won two prestigious awards for its scientific work, which is carried out by both Ugandan and Western scientists.

Reynolds has been studying humans and chimps for 40 years. Does he feel it is possible for the two species to live together peacefully? "Yes, if people are prevented from invading the chimpanzees' space. They have to be prevented by laws, and these laws have to be enforced. At present, enforcement is lacking in Uganda and many other countries."

As in other African countries, Uganda's lush rainforests are shrinking. Yet a recent survey by the Wildlife Conservation Society found that they are still home to nearly 5,000 chimpanzees.

We should give captive chimps proper care and interesting things to do, Reynolds says, and not use them for medical experiments. "In the wild, we have to be careful not to get too close to them, as we can pass on diseases that can kill them.

"We need to give them the respect they deserve as our closest living relatives in the animal kingdom."

APES ON THE MENU

Chimpanzees have only two natural predators—leopards and humans. All over Africa, many people eat "bushmeat"—the flesh of all kinds of wild animals, including endangered ones such as chimps.

∧ Bags of bushmeat will travel on a timber train to city markets and restaurants.

Chimpanzees look so much like humans that many people are discouraged from eating them. Others believe their meat is strengthening, because chimps are so strong. In some areas, chimp bones and hair are used in medicines, and heads and hands are sold as magical objects. But in most of Africa, apes are simply a good source of protein, like any other meat.

Still, until a few years ago, human hunting never threatened the apes with extinction. Today, hunting and deforestation have the potential to wipe out all of Africa's great apes in our lifetime.

What has changed? Africa's population is growing, and more people are living in cities. A multimillion-dollar industry has developed to feed city dwellers who regard bushmeat as a delicacy and pay more for it than beef. While most bushmeat is eaten in Africa, it's been found as far away as London and New York.

The rise in African logging since the 1980s has made it possible to supply this market. To get their huge tree-cutting machines to the timber, companies must build new roads into the forests. These roads make it easy for hunters to reach parts of the forest that were once inaccessible. Loggers, too, hunt for bushmeat, and smuggle it to the city among the logs on their trucks.

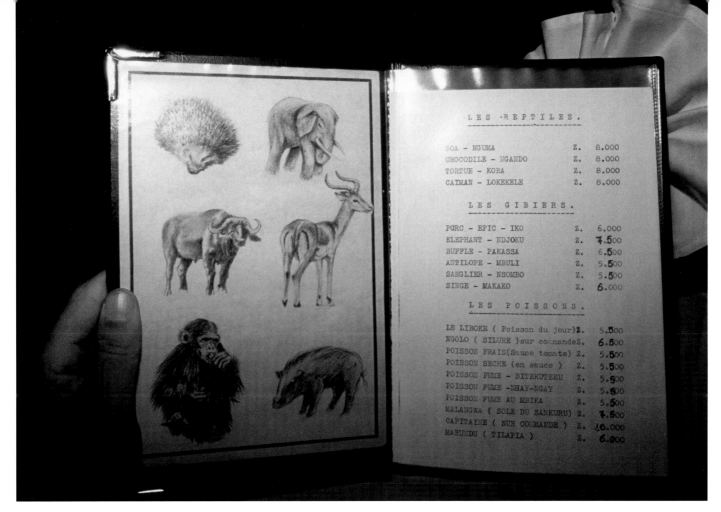

LES ·REPTILES·

BOA — NGUMA	Z.	8.000
CROCODILE — NGANDO	Z.	8.000
TORTUE — KOBA	Z.	8.000
CAIMAN — LOKEKELE	Z.	8.000

LES GIBIERS·

PORC — EPIC — IKO	Z.	6.000
ELEPHANT — NDJOKU	Z.	7.500
BUFFLE — PAKASSA	Z.	6.500
ANTILOPE — MBULI	Z.	5.500
SANGLIER — NSOMBO	Z.	5.500
SINGE — MAKAKO	Z.	6.000

LES POISSONS·

LE LIBOKE (Poisson du jour)	Z.	5.500
NGOLO (SILURE)sur commande	Z.	6.500
POISSON FRAIS(Sauce tomate)	Z.	5.500
POISSON SECHE (en sauce)	Z.	5.500
POISSON FUME — BITEKUTEKU	Z.	5.500
POISSON FUME —NBAY-NGAY	Z.	5.500
POISSON FUME AU MBIKA	Z.	5.500
MALANGWA (SOLE DU SANKURU)	Z.	7.500
CAPITAINE (SUR COMMANDE)	Z.	10.000
MABUNDU (TILAPIA)	Z.	6.000

Chimps, elephants, and crocodiles are all on the menu in a tourist restaurant in Kinshasa, Democratic Republic of Congo.

As many as 4,000 chimpanzees are killed for food each year. Although this is only a fraction of the total bushmeat harvest, chimps have been hit especially hard. Their curiosity about humans makes them easy to spot and kill. They reproduce slowly: a female chimp may have only two or three surviving children in her lifetime. And their close-knit social organization means that it's rarely just one chimp that's lost to the group. A dead alpha male means a disrupted community, and a dead adult female usually means one or two young are taken captive. In smaller groups, it takes very few deaths to put the whole population into a tailspin.

SHUTTING DOWN THE HUNT

In April 2003, officials in Cameroon announced that any restaurant owner caught serving meat from endangered animals could be fined more than $16,000 (U.S.) and jailed for three years. It is a stern law in this central African country, where bushmeat is widely eaten and hunters can earn up to $1,000 a year—nearly twice the average income.

Conservationists agree that tough measures are needed to stop the slaughter. All African countries where great apes live have made it illegal to hunt, eat or sell apes. Unfortunately, however, those laws are often not enforced.

Clearly, the problems at the root of bushmeat hunting—poverty and government inaction—are complex. Conservationists have tackled the problem in many ways, from lobbying governments to enforce laws, to creating publicity campaigns against eating bushmeat, to helping logging companies find alternative food sources for their workers.

Tough measures are needed to stop the slaughter.

In Ivory Coast, a local theater troupe stages dramas in village squares, with the message that chimpanzees are too much like people to be killed for food. In the Democratic Republic of Congo, another group promotes the same message about bonobos by distributing children's books. Programs in Guinea, Cameroon and other countries turn former hunters into educators, field assistants and park guards, providing much-needed jobs while also protecting wildlife.

There will always be people who hunt illegally. To discourage them, armed guards patrol the forests in many countries. This approach is controversial, even among conservationists; many argue that it's wrong to answer violence with more violence. But some feel it's the only effective answer.

< In Tanzania, armed guards patrol protected areas. Some conservationists say it's wrong to use weapons to protect the animals from poachers, others say it's the only effective way.

PRIMATE PEACEMAKERS

Until 1933, bonobos were thought to be a smaller subspecies of chimps, which is why the name pygmy (or dwarf) chimpanzee is still common. Bonobos are now considered a separate species, *Pan paniscus*, which branched off from the chimpanzee family tree about two million years ago. With just 3,000 to 10,000 in the wild, they are also the rarest and most reclusive of the great apes. They're found only in an area of dense rainforest south of the Congo River, in the Democratic Republic of Congo.

They're less warlike than chimpanzees, they're more likely to socialize than fight.

Scientists are fascinated by the behavior of bonobos. Females, rather than males, rule their society. They use sex to reduce tensions and prevent conflict—for example, bonobos will mate briefly when a squabble starts to get nasty. They're less warlike than chimpanzees, they don't hunt animals for food and, when neighboring groups of bonobos meet, they're more likely to socialize than fight.

But these rare apes, which numbered some 100,000 in 1980, are today fast disappearing. Illegal hunting is the main culprit, and the situation was made even worse by a civil war that devastated the country between 1997 and 2002. The war brought extreme poverty and hunger, leaving many people with no choice but to hunt for bushmeat. Even the Mongo people, who once had a taboo against eating bonobos, were driven to abandon it.

Today, with logging companies again pushing roads into the woods, bonobos are increasingly falling prey to poachers. Unless illegal hunting stops, the most recently identified great ape may be the first to become extinct.

S alonga National Park in the Democratic Republic of Congo is one of the world's largest rainforest parks. It's also among the most remote. The only way in is along the river: a three-day trip by motorized dugout canoe.

∧ The ZSM research team at Etate, in Salonga National Park. Once a poachers' camp, Etate is now a base for studying the nearby bonobo population.

Salonga was protected in 1970 to shelter the bonobos, but the laws have not been enforced. "Salonga has always been a hunting ground," says Gay Reinartz of the Zoological Society of Milwaukee (ZSM), the first group to seek out, study and estimate the number of bonobos in the park.

In 1997, the ZSM and a Congolese organization formed the Bonobo and Congo Biodiversity Initiative (BCBI) to find out whether Salonga really was a bonobo stronghold worth conserving. Almost at once they found large groups of bonobos—but also a lot of poaching.

Within months, Congo's civil war halted the project, and life got worse for the apes. Troops were fighting just east of the park, and they needed to be fed. The bonobos were easy prey.

When the research staff returned in October 2000, they were relieved to find more bonobos than they'd expected. But they also found poachers' camps, traps and shotgun shells. The remaining park guards were unpaid, untrained and poorly equipped. Outside Salonga, bushmeat and baby bonobos were being sold in the markets.

The BCBI swung back into action, and now their goals included curbing illegal hunting. One of their first projects was to stretch a cable across the Yenga River to keep poachers from entering by boat. This plan was so effective that it will be a model for future patrols on other rivers. The guards are now being paid regularly, and in 2003 nearly 60 took part in a training program to improve their skills.

Not that the bushmeat problem is solved. "The poachers still occupy sections of the park," Reinartz says. But the BCBI has made a difference. Soon after the war, an abandoned poachers' camp was converted to a patrol post. Eighteen months later, bonobos were seen again in that part of the forest.

∧ TOP In Salonga the rivers are the only roads, and travel is by pirogue (dugout canoe).

BOTTOM Wet shoes dried over the campfire and tents for sleeping are the norm for researchers in Salonga.

The civil war in the Democratic Republic of Congo was in full swing. Inogwabini Bila-Isia and his team of assistants never knew what to expect when they arrived at a military checkpoint. They'd had many tense moments, but this was different.

∧ Inogwabini Bila-Isia demonstrates how poachers set snares.

"It was the first time someone deliberately pointed his gun at me," Bila-Isia says. "He did not understand why, during the war, there were 'crazy people' who, instead of caring for human hardships, were talking about saving 'monkeys.' It's not every day that one survives such moments in a torn-apart country like my homeland."

Frightening though it was, the incident didn't stop Bila-Isia, then director of the BCBI's projects in Salonga National Park, from checking up on the bonobos and park staff alike.

Bila-Isia traces his love of the forest and its creatures to boyhood hunting and fishing trips with his father in the wilderness of northwest Congo. The young Inogwabini had no taste for hunting, but he had a keen eye for the shapes and colors of fish, and an ear for bird calls.

Later, as a university student, he decided he wanted a career in conservation. He studied gorillas and elephants in his native country, got a master's degree from Kent University in England, and then returned home to Salonga and the BCBI.

One way to know if an area of the rainforest is likely to support many bonobos is to survey their food sources, like these leafy marantaceae plants.

Today Bila-Isia helps run a Wildlife Conservation Society project known as MIKE, for Monitoring of Illegal Killing of Elephants. Despite its name, he explains, MIKE is not only about elephants. "We have sites in six countries where our survey teams collect information on both elephants and great apes." Salonga National Park is one of the sites. When the survey is complete, it will be the first reliable picture of where bonobos live throughout Salonga, a first step toward planning for their future.

CHIMPS BEHIND BARS

From the 1950s to the early 1970s, thousands of young chimps were captured in the wild and exported to the developed world. As few as one in five survived the trip.

So endearingly human-like, chimpanzees were sought after as pets and as comic relief in ads, movies and circus shows. And, again because of their likeness to humans, chimps were used as lab subjects in military and medical research.

That has changed. Since 1975, it has been illegal to import wild chimpanzees to most countries, and most research chimps are born in captivity. But the live trade continues. There is still a flourishing—and illegal—international market for baby chimps as exotic pets and entertainers. Huge profits keep the trade alive. An infant chimpanzee that costs $50 (U.S.) in an African village will fetch $30,000 to $40,000 in the United States. A buyer may never know whether that cute baby chimp was bred in captivity, or taken from the body of its dead mother in the forest.

When police or customs officers catch chimp smugglers in Africa, rescued chimpanzees—usually babies orphaned by the bushmeat trade—are taken to sanctuaries. The number of orphans has risen steeply in recent years, though, and most primate sanctuaries are now bursting at the seams.

While life in a sanctuary is better than being chained or locked in a cage, it's still a long leap from freedom. And it's not cheap to shelter a chimp, even in Africa. It can cost $2,000 (U.S.) or more per year to keep each animal, and they can live as long as 50 years. Some conservationists argue that the money would be better spent battling habitat loss and bushmeat hunting.

^ Movies like *Tarzan* created a false image of chimpanzees as perfect pets—small, friendly, comical, and cute.

< These young chimps are just three of hundreds of new orphans crowding African sanctuaries today.

LIFE UNDER THE BIG TOP

Before World War II, any circus worthy of the name would have had a chimpanzee act. Animal acts are no longer as popular as they once were in North American circuses, but you can still catch an occasional chimp performance. Dressed in clown suits, pedaling miniature bicycles, strumming guitars or walking on stilts and flashing that toothy grin, chimps seem to enjoy the show as much as the spectators do.

Unfortunately, like so much in show business, the happy-go-lucky circus chimp is an illusion. Training begins when they are very young, when chimps in the wild would still be clinging to their mothers. Trainers beat the chimps to make them obey, and may pull out their canine teeth so they can't bite. The chimps are housed alone in cramped, barren cages to motivate them to get out and perform. While not all trainers are abusive, and extreme brutality is no longer so common, many trainers still find it faster and easier to handle chimps with force and fear, rather than rewards and praise.

Some circus chimps perform for many years, but more often adulthood brings aggressiveness along with increased strength, making them unmanageable. When this happens, they are hard to place in zoos because they have never learned to get along with other chimps. A few lucky ones find their way into sanctuaries for retired entertainment chimps, but most end up in research labs.

Animal welfare groups in several countries are leading a movement to exclude primates from circuses and animal shows. Chimps are still featured in circuses all over the world, but in a handful of countries—and in some areas of the United States, Canada and the United Kingdom—circuses that use any animals are banned.

< Dressed in human clothing and dancing the conga, these chimps were star circus performers in 1975. Today, many countries have banned circuses with animal acts.

SETTING THEM FREE

If African sanctuaries are overflowing with chimps, why don't they simply let the animals loose in the forest?

To begin with, it can't be just any forest. It must be large enough to provide a wide variety of fruit and other food. There must be no great threat from hunting or logging, and no large human population nearby. It must be part of a large, protected wilderness area or connected to other forested areas, not a fragment of woods where the chimps will become isolated. At the same time, introducing a new group of animals to a large chimp population could spark bitter clashes and loss of life on both sides.

∧ A baby chimp looks out at the world from behind a sanctuary's wire fence.

Even when the release area is ideal, it's no simple matter to send a chimp back to its natural habitat. In the wild, chimps spend up to eight years learning survival skills from their mothers and other adults. They watch grown-ups build sleeping nests, "fish" for termites and crack nuts. Sometimes a mother chimpanzee will actively show her infant the right way to hold a branch, or strike a nut against a stone. It can take five years of practice before a young chimp can obtain food as efficiently as its mother.

In a sanctuary, where humans provide regular meals and protection from leopards and poachers, a chimpanzee grows up healthy and safe, but does not learn to fend for itself. A chimp suddenly dropped off in a forest by itself would be as helpless as a child abandoned in a strange city.

In Chimfunshi Orphanage, Africa's largest chimpanzee sanctuary, chimps lead a > nearly normal life. But even the best sanctuary can't compete with the rainforest as a home for chimpanzees.

The African sanctuary HELP Congo is the only one devoted to returning orphaned chimpanzees to the wild. Its key strategy is to let chimps learn survival skills before setting them free.

The sanctuary was set up in 1991, in the Conkouati Lagoon near the Atlantic coast of the Republic of Congo. The youngest chimps lived in a nursery, where volunteers provided the constant attention and physical contact that baby primates demand. After a few years they were moved to three forest-covered islands, where they practiced getting along with other chimps, building nests and finding food—with as little human contact as possible. By 1994, 48 chimps were living in the sanctuary.

In 1996, the first group made its leap to freedom in the Conkouati Triangle, a wedge of forest covering 8 square miles (21 km²) of a national park. Rich in food, and home to few wild chimpanzees— and even fewer humans—the Triangle was an ideal release site.

By 2003, 37 chimpanzees, all chosen for their good health and survival skills, had been returned to the wild. To keep the population pure, researchers made sure that all the released chimps belonged to the same subspecies, *Pan troglodytes troglodytes*, as those already living in the Triangle.

∧ With a helping hand from a researcher, Derek, a six-year-old male, leaves his cage for the freedom of the Conkouati Triangle.

< HELP Congo's volunteers step in for missing mothers to give the youngest chimps the care and attention they need—including a cuddle at naptime.

Sophie, an adult female chimp, is fitted with a radio collar while under anesthetic. Signals from the collar will let scientists keep track of Sophie without getting too close to her.

It's been a clear success, says scientist Benoît Goossens, president of HELP International. "We have shown that in the right conditions, and following strict guidelines, it's possible to release orphan chimpanzees."

Little Andreas, seen with his mother, Choupette, was the first HELP Congo baby chimp born in the wild. Every wild-born baby is a sign that the freed chimps are doing well.

Researchers monitor the chimps from a distance, reading signals from the radio collars that some of the animals wear. There is a veterinarian on hand to treat injured chimps, though not all have survived accidents, leopard attacks or fights with wild apes. But 65 percent of released chimps are known to be alive—a respectable survival rate. They roam freely between the Triangle and the vast national park, and two of the females have had babies.

> Relocating isolated chimps to larger protected areas could prove a useful conservation tool, Goossens says. "But I don't think that releasing chimpanzees in the wild will save the species," he cautions. "The most important measures are preserving their habitat and protecting them from hunting."

In 1989, French-born businesswoman Aliette Jamart was living in Pointe-Noire, the Republic of Congo, when a friend persuaded her to visit the local zoo. That visit changed her life.

The conditions at the zoo were horrendous. "There were three rows of cages, each more disgusting than the last," Aliette recalls. One of the two baby chimps was so badly nourished that his thighbones had broken through the skin.

∧ Jeannette's wild-born son, Mai, imitates her as she uses a stick to forage for food.

Jamart had no experience with chimpanzees, but she was struck by the "human" look in their eyes. She convinced the authorities to let her take the two babies home and try to restore them to health. The male died, but the female— whom Jamart named Jeannette—survived and grew.

One chimp led to another. When poachers were caught killing chimpanzee mothers, the orphaned babies were taken to Jamart. Within two years, 21 well-fed, energetic young chimps were making themselves at home in her house and yard.

But Jamart was upset with the idea of keeping a wild animal fenced in for its 50-year life span. The chimps would have to go back to the forest, where they belonged.

This was the beginning of HELP Congo. Jamart persuaded the Congolese government to let her create a sanctuary in Conkouati Lagoon, won the support and partnership of several well-known scientists and threw herself into the never-ending task of fundraising.

Since the day in 1989 when Aliette Jamart walked into an ill-kept zoo in Pointe-Noir, Congo, she has devoted her life to returning captive chimps to the wild.

When the first five chimpanzees were released in 1996, Jeannette was among them, and Jamart was there to watch her first orphan go free. In Spring 2003, things came full circle as Jeannette had her first baby, a male named Maî. Mother and child are doing well—so far. And so are most of the other newly freed chimpanzees.

> Jamart is now channeling her energy into making sure the effort won't go to waste. She hopes to build a new research station on the site of the sanctuary. The presence of researchers would discourage poachers, making it a safer place for former captives and their young.

BLURRING THE LINE

When scientists discovered in the 1970s that chimpanzees and humans share most of their genetic identity, they decided that chimps would be useful test subjects for new drugs and medical procedures. Things could be done to them that could not be done to people; some were deliberately infected with diseases.

As the public learned more about chimpanzees, it became difficult for anyone to pretend that the life of a lab chimp was anything but cruel. Often separated from their mothers as babies and caged without activities to stimulate the mind, lab chimps have little or no social contact. But these animals also share much of our intelligence.

In the last 40 years, chimps have even learned to communicate with human language. Washoe, a female chimpanzee at Central Washington University, began learning American Sign Language in 1966. She has mastered 240 signs, even combining them to make up new terms, such as "water bird" for swan.

In the 1980s, a young bonobo named Kanzi learned lexigrams (symbols representing words) and soon had a vocabulary of more than 200, which he combined into sentences using a keyboard. A chimp named Ai, at Japan's Kyoto University, can memorize random numbers and recall them with an accuracy and a speed that often beat graduate students. Great apes have even been known to recognize their own faces in mirrors, proving that they are aware of themselves as individuals.

Today, attitudes about chimpanzees are changing, but a passionate debate continues between those who believe it is wrong to exploit our closest kin, and those who argue that experimenting on chimps can save human lives.

As Jane Goodall has said, "We humans are, of course, unique, but we are not so different from the rest of the animal kingdom as we used to suppose."

< Scientists like Dr. Sue Savage-Rumbaugh of the Language Research Center in Atlanta Georgia, have changed our ideas about ape intelligence. This bonobo chooses symbols from a lexigram board to communicate.

Soon after John Glenn blasted off in *Freedom 7* in 1962, he became the first man to orbit Earth—but he wasn't the first primate to do so. That honor goes to Enos, a five-year-old chimpanzee who flew a similar mission on November 29, 1961.

∧ The "astrochimps" were heros, briefly. Later, chimps in the U.S. Space Program were leased to biomedical labs for drug testing.

The U.S. Air Force needed to test the effects of space flight before humans attempted it, so they used Enos and other young chimps. The "astrochimps" were famous—for a while. Then humans headed into space and the chimps were forgotten. Most ended up in research labs, where they were exposed to cancer-causing chemicals or infected with HIV or hepatitis, then used to test new drugs. Some were caged alone for more than 30 years.

In 1997, the Air Force gave most of its remaining chimpanzees to the Coulston Foundation, a lab in New Mexico that had the country's worst record for the care of its animals. It was charged by the U.S. government four times, more than any other lab, for providing poor living conditions and careless medical treatment causing the deaths of 10 chimpanzees.

When scientist Carole Noon heard about this, she created the Center for Captive Chimpanzee Care (CCCC), and went to court to fight for the chimps. After a long battle, the organization won the release of the chimpanzees from Coulston. The CCCC now cares for 291 chimps—including 36 survivors or descendants of the space program—at its sanctuary in Florida.

Thanks to Dr. Carole Noon, lab chimps like Sinbad are leaving their cages in New Mexico for an open-air life in a Florida sanctuary.

The freed chimps live on a grassy island, where they dine on fresh fruit and vegetables, climb and play or just sit in the sun, grooming each other. Nobody sticks needles in them. Scientists can study them, but only through the use of video monitors.

Many people still don't understand how much like humans chimpanzees are, especially in the ways they socialize. Isolate them from other chimps, and they're miserable. In other words, as Noon says, "Chimpanzees have the same feelings as you and I do."

WHAT IS THE CHIMPANZEE'S FUTURE?

Conservationists agree that the problems facing chimpanzees and the other great apes are enormous—and growing worse. Bushmeat hunting, habitat loss and diseases are taking their toll, and some believe that in just five to ten years they'll be extinct across most of their range.

The problems facing chimpanzees are enormous. But the picture isn't completely bleak.

But the picture isn't completely bleak. In recent years, conservation projects in Africa and new laws in the West have been created to help protect chimpanzees. There seems to be a new willingness among African leaders to recognize the value of conservation—for example, the government of Gabon established 13 national parks in 2002.

Nobody says it will be easy to fend off extinction. Governments need to enforce anti-poaching laws, control logging and spend more money on disease research. And even those efforts may not be enough.

Any successful plan must take human welfare into account; in other words, local people should not just be told to protect the chimps and bonobos, but also made certain that it's in their own best interest to do so.

Can the chimpanzees survive? It's possible, but it will take all the hard work and commitment their human cousins can muster.

The deadliest threat to the survival of chimpanzees comes from human beings.   >
Ironically, the best chance for the chimps' future also lies in human hands.

FAST FACTS

Scientific name	• *Pan troglodytes* (chimpanzee, abbreviated *P.t.* below) and *Pan paniscus* (bonobo)
Subspecies	• *P.t. verus* (western); *P.t. troglodytes* (central); *P.t. schweinfurthii* (eastern); *P.t. vellerosus* (Nigeria/Cameroon)
Size	• adult male chimps weigh 75 to 155 pounds (34 to 70 kg); adult male bonobos weigh 75 to 100 lb (34 to 45 kg)
	• both stand 3.5 to 5.5 feet (1 to 1.7 m)
	• arm span up to 8 feet (2.4 m)
	• males are 25 to 30 percent larger than females
Life span	• 40 to 50 years in the wild; up to 60 years in zoos
Locomotion	• walk with feet flat on ground and arms resting on knuckles
	• may walk upright for short distances while carrying objects or showing dominance
	• long, strong arms allow for swinging through trees to find food and escape predators
	• opposable thumbs on hands and feet allow for tool making and other manual tasks
Communication	• most distinctive chimp call is the pant-hoot: a loud, excited call made when finding food or meeting others; can be heard up to two miles (3.2 km) away
	• bonobos make quieter but more frequent barking noises
	• gestures used more than vocalization to communicate

Reproduction •   will mate year-round
  •   females begin to reproduce at about age 13
      and every four to six years afterward
  •   gestation lasts approximately 230 days;
      single births usual, twins are rare
  •   babies have pale faces that later darken and
      white tail tufts that vanish after four or five years
  •   young may nurse for up to four years

Senses •   rely on sight more than smell
  •   red-blue-green color vision—like most
      primates but unlike any other mammals

Social life •   small groups form and disperse within larger
      community
  •   males stay to guard territory, females migrate
  •   male chimps dominate; female bonobos dominate
  •   lifelong bonds kept between friends and family members
  •   grooming is a form of social bonding

HOW YOU CAN HELP

If you would like to learn more about chimpanzees and bonobos, and the projects designed to protect them, contact one of the following organizations or visit their Web sites.

Bonobo and Congo Biodiversity Initiative
www.zoosociety.org

c/o Zoological Society of Milwaukee, 10005 West Blue Mound Road, Milwaukee, WI, U.S.A. 53226
Phone (414) 258-2333
Includes information on bonobos and on the BCBI's efforts to save them.

Budongo Forest Project
www.budongo.org

P.O. Box 362, Masindi, Uganda
Describes the project's research and includes online newsletter.

The Bushmeat Project
bushmeat.net

P.O. Box 3430, Palos Verdes, CA, U.S.A. 90274
Phone (310) 377-0317
Shares information about the great ape bushmeat problem.

Center for Captive Chimpanzee Care
www.savethechimps.org

P.O. Box 12220, Fort Pierce, FL, U.S.A. 34979
Phone (772) 429-0403
Tells the story of the Astrochimps and their lives today in the sanctuary.

Bossou Environmental Research Institute
www.pri.kyoto-u.ac.jp/chimp

Primate Research Institute, Kyoto University, 41 Kanrin, Inuyama, Aichi, Japan 484-8506
Includes detailed information on the Bossou field study and chimpanzee behavior, especially their use of tools.

Friends of Washoe
www.friendsofwashoe.org

Chimpanzee & Human Communication Institute, Central Washington University, 400 East 8th Avenue, Ellensburg, WA, U.S.A. 98926-7573
Phone (509) 963-2244
Provides information about Washoe and other chimps learning American Sign Language.

HELP International
www.help-primates.org

26, rue du Capitaine Ferber, 75020 Paris, France
Features a photo gallery and details on reintroducing chimps to the wild.

Jane Goodall Institute
www.janegoodall.org

8700 Georgia Avenue, Suite 500, Silver Spring, MD, U.S.A. 20910-3605
Phone (301) 565-0086
Covers all aspects of chimp conservation, with links to U.S. and Canadian branches and to the institute's youth wing, Roots & Shoots.

INDEX

PHOTO CREDITS

front cover: Gerry Ellis/Minden Pictures
back cover: Latour Stephanie/Corbis/Magma
p. 2   Gerry Ellis/Minden Pictures
p. 6   Gerry Ellis/Minden Pictures

p. 10   Bettman/Corbis/Magma
p. 11   Kennan Ward/Corbis/Magma
p. 12   Gallo Images/Corbis/Magma
p. 15   Kennan Ward/Corbis/Magma
p. 16–19 Tetsuno Matsuzawa
p. 21   Global Forest Watch/World
         Resources Institute
p. 22   Staffan Widstrand/Magma/Corbis
p. 23   Karl Ammann
p. 24   Karl Ammann
p. 25   Frans Lanting/Minden Pictures
p. 26   courtesy of Budongo Forest Project
p. 27   Frans Lanting/Minden Pictures
p. 28   Gerry Ellis/Minden Pictures
p. 29   Art Wolfe/Photo Researchers
p. 30–31 Karl Ammann
p. 32   Richard Smith/Corbis/Magma
p. 35   Frans Lanting/Minden Pictures
p. 36–39 courtesy of Bonobo and Congo
         Biodiversity Initiative
p. 40   Karl Ammann/Corbis/Magma
p. 41   Bettman/Corbis/Magma
p. 42   Henry Diltz/Corbis/Magma
p. 44   Karl Ammann/Corbis/Magma
p. 45   Gallo Images/Corbis/Magma
p. 46   Latour Stephanie/Corbis/Magma
p. 47   Joanna Setchell & Benoit
         Goossens/HELP
p. 48   Latour Stephanie/Corbis/Magma
p. 49   Carmen Vidal/HELP
p. 50   Benoit Goossens/HELP
p. 51   Latour Stephanie/Corbis/Magma
p. 52   Frans Lanting/Minden Pictures
p. 54   Bettman/Corbis/Magma
p. 55   Dean Hanson/The Albuquerque
         Journal/AP
p. 57   Gerry Ellis/Minden Pictures
p. 59   Joanna Setchell & Benoit
         Goossens/HELP

AUTHOR'S NOTE

Thanks are due to the experts who were so generous with their knowledge and expertise, especially Tetsuro Matsuzawa, Lee White, Vernon Reynolds, Gay Reinartz, Inogwabini Bila-Isia, Benoît Goossens, Aliette Jamart and Carole Noon.